20 BEST IDEAS

To Generate Profitable Passive Income and Build Wealth In 2022 & Beyond

ROBERT J. PENN

All rights reserved.

No part of this publication may be reproduced, distributed, or transmitted in any form or by any means, including photocopying, recording, or other electronic or mechanical methods, without the prior written permission of the publisher, except in the case of brief quotations embodied in critical reviews and certain other noncommercial uses permitted by copyright law.

Copyright © by Robert J. Penn 2022

TABLE OF CONTENTS

CHAPTER 4

CONCLUSION

CHAPTER 1

Introduction

We frequently portray passive income as *"making money while you rest,"* but there's more to it than that.

Assuming it truly was that simple, everybody would count dollar notes while also counting sheep.

Assuming you have sufficient cash, you can purchase resources like an Airbnb investment property, digital currency, and stocks that bring in money on autopilot. But, what happens if you don't have the resources to get everything rolling?

Even though it gets promoted as easy money, passive income ideas are the result of hard work: building an audience of ready buyers; optimizing paid advertisements, and delivering an extraordinary experience and an unrivaled product.

However, as a current or hopeful entrepreneur, you won't hesitate to invest the effort to do those things, and you could, as of now, have each of the three marked off your list.

Adding passive income sources to your life can give you more freedom, opportunity, flexibility, and cash.

The answer for some individuals is to make the assets themselves.

Greater resources, similar to property, include investment capital that not every person has, but creating assets yourself demands your time and effort as an investment, so you can receive the benefits later.

Passive income can be an incredible method for helping you with producing additional income, whether you're running a side hustle or simply attempting to get some extra dough every month, particularly considering the widespread economic inflation.

Passive income can assist you with earning during the good times and tide you over if you become unemployed, if you intentionally take some time away from work, or if inflation keeps reducing your purchasing power.

With passive income, you can have cash coming in even as you pursue your primary job, or if you're able to generate a strong stream of passive income, you should be able to kick back a bit.

One way or the other, a passive income gives you additional security.

Furthermore, if you're stressed over having the option to save enough of your profit to meet your retirement objectives, creating wealth through passive income is a strategy that could suit you well.

Passive income can be an amazing long-term income stream and a reliable cash flow.

Here is a guide to passive income for newbies.

CHAPTER 2

What Is Passive Income?

We define passive income as active unearned pay that requires little or no work to create and keep up with and comes from somewhere other than a traditional employer.

Recurring earnings from a source other than an employer or contractor are considered passive income.

Passive income sources include mutual fund investments, selling items online, online course teaching on websites, and other auxiliary jobs that don't require active participation. These are examples of passive income sources.

Passive income generates unearned residual revenue with little time and effort. You'll have more time, and your finances will improve.

Not being able to trade your time for cash can relieve pressure and uneasiness and can cause you to have high expectations of your financial future.

Whether you're running a service provider attempting to quit selling money for time or a product business hoping to add income streams that don't require the hassle of conveying actual goods, look at the following passive income strategies.

Passive Income Isn't...

i. <u>Your Job:</u> Generally, passive income isn't pay that comes from something you've been actively engaged with, like the paychecks you earn from a job.

ii. <u>Your Second Job:</u> Finding a second line of work won't qualify as a passive income since you'll still have to be present and accomplish the work to get paid.

Passive income means building a reliable stream of income without you doing a ton of work to get it.

iii. <u>Non-income-producing assets:</u> Investing can be an extraordinary method for producing passive income, provided that the resources you own deliver profits or interest.

Non-profit-paying stocks or resources like cryptocurrency might be stimulating, but they will not earn you passive income.

An In-Depth Analysis of Passive Income.

With passive income, you're not trading your time for cash, as you could do at a regular job.

Instead, you're creating or purchasing an asset that you can sell or produce income with, whether or not you're at your work area or on the ocean side in the Maldives.

There are a lot of passive income ideas, such as writing a book, creating a course, putting resources into a landed property or real estate, and running an affiliate marketing program.

However, these exercises are generally not quite as passive as individuals like to think. You need to invest the energy upfront, such as writing the book you will sell, shooting the videos for your course, and picking the assets you'll purchase.

Also, you need to do either of these without getting directly paid, with the expectation that it will pay off for months or years subsequently.

Passive income frequently includes some extra work en route, as well.

You might need to keep your products updated or your assets well maintained to keep the free dollars pouring in.

Regardless of this, passive income can be a pleasant extra income stream (something that has never been more significant in a precarious and recuperating economy).

What Are The Various Sorts Of Passive Income?

Unearned pay comes in **two principal forms**. Each one gives an alternate method for creating income, and they can be utilized separately or in pairs, depending on your financial objectives:

1. <u>Creating:</u> We earn money from doing the work proactively.

Examples of passive income include freelancing, selling digital products, writing books, making music, or making another item that brings in money.

2. <u>Investing:</u> We earn money from asset investments.

Dividend stocks, real estate investment trusts, leasing or renting out a spare room, interest, capital gains, peer loaning, mutual funds, and royalty payments are some examples of investments that often involve an initial cost.

What Distinguishes Passive Income From Active Income?

The primary distinction between active and passive income is that active income is obtained via output or effort. In contrast, passive income needs implementation and research.

Both kinds of income require work; it's simply an instance of when that work occurs.

While someone who creates 10 blog articles in advance for their website and monetizes them with affiliate links is generating passive income, someone who is paid by a company to generate blog material each month is generating earned income.

Earned income is the traditional income model since it doesn't have as many dangers.

The idea is straightforward: you accomplish the tasks for which you get paid.

For creatives and social media influencers with full-time jobs or other duties who want to continue growing their brand, passive income is a great side hustle.

The Advantages Of Passive Income.

1. <u>Acquire Extra Income:</u>

Conceivable wealth creation is the big draw of passive income.

It can give you an alternative wealth choice, speed up early retirement, support a nomadic way of life, and raise your net worth.

By setting up several passive income sources, you may avoid being dependent on a single one that might fail at any time.

2. <u>Greater Financial Liberty</u>:

Earning additional money is only one aspect of passive income.

You may make enough money to cover your living needs without working or depending on others if you have enough sources of income.

Additionally, it provides you the freedom to use your time any way you see fit, whether that be pursuing side projects or establishing a small business.

3. <u>Lessens Tension And Anxiety</u>:

One of the main sources of worry for people is not having enough money to cover their expenses.

You won't have to worry about not having enough money to cover your bills if you are earning passive income.

Generating passive income gives you the financial momentum you need to handle your money, your time, and your assets responsibly.

4. <u>It Makes It Possible For You To Live And Work Wherever You Choose</u>:

When you are not dependent on a paycheck, you can live and work anywhere.

You can't achieve the freedom through other means of making money that passive income can.

You can travel or partake in other activities while working remotely as long as you maintain your standard of living.

5. <u>You Can More Easily Achieve Your Goals:</u>

Even though money cannot buy everything, it can certainly purchase a lot.

Additionally, having passive assets gives you access to extra money.

That implies that you have more extra money to set aside for investments and savings, which are crucial steps toward achieving financial freedom.

In other words, your passive income accelerates the achievement of your goals.

6. <u>You May Retire Earlier:</u>

Many people eagerly anticipate their retirement. However, if you're still living paycheck to paycheck, retirement is most likely still far off.

You may begin saving for retirement earlier if you have a passive income.

That enables you to enjoy your golden years and retire early!

One of the greatest and most crucial components of a stable financial status is passive income.

I haven't seen a single drawback to passive income, from increasing your financial security to lowering your financial stress.

Passive Income: How Much Could You Earn?

There isn't a maximum or minimum amount of passive income you can earn.

Depending on the value and scalability of the product you're selling, it can range from a few additional cents a month to hundreds of thousands of dollars a year.

For instance, you may anticipate a return of 10.5% a year if you invest in an ETF that tracks the S&P 500.

The average annual return on residential rental properties is 7.5%, whereas the average annual return on industrial real estate investments is 9.5%.

When compared to high-yield savings accounts, which may offer you up to 1.5% annually, these returns are significantly greater.

Passive income is another way for online content creators to support themselves. Frankie Calkins, a personal finance YouTuber, and author made $800 in passive income in January from the sale of books, affiliate marketing, and advertising on her YouTube channel. Another person made more than $100,000 from dropshipping ($6,000 from the sale of a plush elephant pillow for babies alone).

One of Udemy's highest-paid instructors earns about $17,000 each month selling online courses.

The amount of time, money, and resources you invest in developing your product, its scalability, the price you're charging, and the level of demand all have an impact on your revenue.

Why Is Passive Income Significant For Organizations?

Businesses that generate passive income can expand their wealth and cash flow, which increases their financial security and stability.

In practice, passive income boosts overall earnings, saves time, and broadens the market for a company.

Passive revenue makes location independence possible for certain business owners, as is the case with digital nomads.

Less stress, more time to pursue interests and initiatives, and an earlier retirement are some additional advantages of passive income.

But keep in mind that before passive money starts to flow in, a substantial amount of effort must be spent pursuing active revenue sources, sometimes for years.

Is Passive Income Taxable?

The *Internal Revenue Service (IRS)* has opinions on passive and residual income, as it does with anything monetary.

You must still be aware of and follow regional income tax regulations:

Become familiar with the Internal Revenue Service's definition of passive income: *"Net rental income" or "revenue from a company in which the taxpayer does not significantly participate"* are the two definitions of passive income.

The IRS has a series of rules for what it defines as *"material involvement,"* which evaluates whether someone has actively participated in business or another activity that generates money.

Understand when passive income is taxed.

A hint: It's always. Although it is often taxed at the same rate as salary, the IRS may handle it differently.

This isn't meant to be tax or financial advice. I recommend that you speak with an accountant to discuss your case.

There Is Work In Real Passive Income.

It's critical to acknowledge passive income for what it is—work—when considering it. It may be possible for you to do it on the weekends and at night, but it still demands labor.

Even if it makes money while you are occupied with other activities, it still demands labor.

Profit from a job is not passive. Work is required for passive income. Occasionally, a lot of labor.

One advantage that passive income has over full-time employment is that it separates work from pleasure. When you show up for work in a 9 to 5 job, you are paid.

Your employer will cease paying you if you quit showing up.

People focus on ways to make money without working when they consider passive income. That could be true, but it's not accurate.

Simply put, *individuals are getting money for labor they previously completed while engaging in other activities.*

When you make stock market investments, you put in the initial research now and benefit afterward. It might happen months, years, or even decades later.

The idea that hard work pays off is another misconception. Not all efforts result in rewards. Losses, perhaps enormous losses, may result.

The main point is that *making an effort may result in enormous benefits as well.*

A blog may be created from nothing and sold for millions of dollars.

You won't get wealthy overnight, but you could get there sooner than you think (and poorer too).

Therefore, keep in mind that the goal of passive income is to *detach effort from reward.*

When you sleep, it is not free money.

CHAPTER 3

Passive Income Ideas

Here is our list of 20 passive income ideas to help you start earning at least $1,000 a month if you're thinking about doing so.

You'll understand the requirements for success with them as well as the risks associated with each idea.

Some may need an initial time or work commitment, but after the project is finished, they can continue to earn you cash passively and indefinitely.

1. <u>Create A Course.</u>

One popular method to get passive income is to create an audio or video course, then sit back and watch the money roll in from the sale of your product.

You probably possess extensive expertise on a subject that others are eager to pay for. Try developing courses with that knowledge in mind.

The entrance hurdle is low, and you frequently don't need to make an initial financial commitment.

The sale and distribution of courses are made possible by websites like *Udemy, SkillShare, and Coursera.*

Online courses are similar to digital goods in that you may sell them repeatedly without keeping any stock or inventory.

An alternative is to use a *"freemium model,"* which comprises building an audience with free content and afterward charging for in-depth knowledge or for individuals who desire to know more.

For example, stock-picking advisors and language instructors might both employ this strategy. The free content showcases your skills and can attract individuals seeking to advance their careers.

The greatest method to increase sales of a current product is to produce additional top-notch goods.

A course can provide a great source of revenue because you may quickly generate money after your first investment.

You can create a reliable income stream once you have mastered the business model.

2. <u>Sell Digital Assets.</u>

Digital products are assets or media that customers can't physically touch and feel. They are intangible resources.

These consist of files that we can download or stream, such as *PDFs, templates, plug-ins, or e-books* like the one you're reading right now.

The high-profit margins of digital products make them excellent passive income generators. The item simply has to be created once, and you may sell it online frequently.

Inventory or storage space is not required. You are free to sell as many digital products as you like.

By offering professional-use kits, printouts, files, and other resources for sale, many designers increase their passive revenue.

To help with the design process, UX Kits, for example, sell personas, flowcharts, and wireframes.

Writing an e-book may be a great way to benefit from the low cost of publication and even from the global reach of platforms like *Amazon* to get your book in front of potentially millions of prospective readers.

Since they rely on your skills, e-books may be created for relatively little money and have a length of 30 to 50 pages.

An e-book may serve as a vehicle for directing readers to your other products, such as audio or video courses, additional e-books, a website, or perhaps more valuable seminars, in addition to providing them with useful information and value.

You'll need to be an authority on a certain subject, although it's possible that the subject is niche and calls for specialized knowledge or talents that few possess but that many people desire.

On an online platform, you can quickly create the book and test-market several titles and pricing points.

However, most of the value comes when you include more e-books in the mix, bringing in more readers to your material, much like when developing a course.

3. __Rental Income.__

Renting out real estate is an excellent strategy to generate passive income. But more effort than individuals expect is frequently required.

You risk losing your investment if you don't take the time to learn how to make it profitable.

One of the earliest methods of creating long-term wealth is real estate investing.

If you have enough money, you may buy and rent out apartment complexes or other types of real estate.

However, because being a landlord is a somewhat active profession, you can engage property managers to handle tenants and gather rent or monthly payments.

You must decide on three (3) factors in getting passive revenue from rental properties:

➤ The desired rate of return on investment.
➤ The entire cost and expenses for the property.
➤ The costs associated with owning the property.

For instance, if your goal is to generate $10,000 a year in rental income and the property has a $2,000 monthly mortgage, as well as an additional $300 a month in taxes and other charges,

To meet your goal, you would need to charge $3,133 in rent each month.

4. **Establish A Print-On-Demand Business.**

Print on demand may be a viable passive income concept and a way to monetize your creativity if you're an artist, designer, or business owner.

Working with suppliers, it entails customizing white-label items like *t-shirts, posters, backpacks, or books,* then offering them for sale based on individual orders.

You simply have to pay for the product once you sell it, much like dropshipping. No inventories or large purchases are required. Print-on-demand businesses are excellent sources of passive income because:

You can create products quickly and place them up for sale in a matter of minutes.

Your supplier handles fulfillment and shipping.

You may automate numerous marketing and sales procedures once you set up your store.

You can quickly and simply produce things to sell in your *Shopify store* using a print-on-demand firm like *Printful.*

You can also sell goods with your designs on websites like *CafePress* and *Zazzle,* including T-shirts, caps, mugs, and more.

Overall, print on demand is a low-risk, straightforward business idea that you can implement quickly.

Starting with your creations, you may gauge the market's interest before expanding.

You might be able to take advantage of growing interest in a current issue and create a shirt that, at the very least, offers a sarcastic take on it.

Additionally, you may create your online storefront to sell your goods using a website like Shopify.

5. <u>Launch A Business In Affiliate Marketing.</u>

Recommending a product or service to an audience is the major component of affiliate marketing.

Since you earn a commission every time someone uses your referral link to purchase the suggested item or service, it's a fantastic passive revenue source.

It is a sector that is expanding. By 2022, Statista predicts the affiliate marketing industry to be worth $8.2 billion.

The most popular affiliate partner might be Amazon, but other well-known brands include *eBay, Awin, JV Zoo, and ShareASale.*

Also, *Facebook, Instagram, and TikTok* have grown to be enormous platforms for those trying to build a following and advertise their goods.

For the following main reasons, online business owners become affiliate marketers:

a. <u>It is easy to execute.</u> You only take care of the marketing aspect of things. The company will create items and complete orders.

b. <u>Low risk applies.</u> Joining an affiliate platform is completely free. You can sell current profits with no initial outlay of cash.

You'll need to put some work into developing traffic sources to increase the number of clicks on your links. Once that's done, commissions are a pretty passive source of income.

c. <u>You can scale it.</u> Typically, affiliate marketers don't employ additional staff. While your prior work generates income in the background, you may present new goods to an audience and design campaigns.

Making money with affiliate marketing may be a satisfying way to expand the sources of income for your business.

Your time is the only expense. Once the hours are put in, you will continue to reap the benefits.

6. <u>Market Homemade Products.</u>

Online sales have never been more profitable. The chance to create and grow an online business is enormous given that there are already over 4.6 billion internet users worldwide.

You can sell on hundreds of online sites. Some, like video games or handcrafted products, have defined niches, whilst others allow you to sell anything you choose.

Popular online marketplaces include:

- ➠ Your online store (if you have any).
- ➠ Handshake.

- ➠ Amazon.
- ➠ eBay.
- ➠ Ruby Lane.
- ➠ AliExpress.

This is a double upfront investment. Making and selling handmade items like pottery or clothes will require an investment of both time and resources.

Our study indicates that the top ten items that customers want to purchase post-pandemic are as follows:

- ✓ Infant items and clothing.
- ✓ Virtual events and classes.
- ✓ Exercise equipment.
- ✓ Items for cleaning the home.
- ✓ Beautifying products (e.g., skincare, haircare, etc.).
- ✓ Products for personal care (e.g., toothpaste, soap, etc.).
- ✓ Groceries.
- ✓ Athleisure clothes.
- ✓ Clothing items (e.g., shoes, hats, etc.).
- ✓ Pet products.

Selling from your store allows you to build a name for yourself while reducing the amount of fees you spend on each transaction.

The advantages of creating a brand compound over time as you expand your audience and establish relationships with new clients. You'll sell more over time and increase your online income.

7. <u>Sell Stock Photographs On The Web.</u>

The fact that you get paid for your time when you run a service-based business like photography is one of its biggest drawbacks.

To make money with photography, you must be present at an event or photo session, which might get tiresome after a while, even if you're making a fortune.

Although selling photography online may not appear to be the most obvious approach to begin a passive income stream, if you can sell the same photographs frequently, you may be able to scale your efforts.

If you have a nice camera or work as a full-time photographer, you may sell your images online to get an extra income.

Stock photo websites like *Pexels, Shutterstock,* and other online media firms will pay you for high-quality images and videos.

You'll need images that speak to a specific audience or capture a particular scenario, and you'll need to figure out where the market is.

Photographs might be of models, landscapes, creative scenes, and more, or they could record actual occurrences that the media might cover.

Except for your camera and laptop, there is nothing else you need to have around the house.

Once you upload your images to the platform, these websites will handle the marketing for you, allowing you to focus on selling your work.

If you operate your photography business on Shopify, you can simply link digital items like prints or print-on-demand products like shirts and caps, offering you even more passive income streams as a result of which you may work less and earn more.

The ability to expand your efforts is one of the benefits of selling or licensing your photos through a platform, especially if you can produce images that will be in demand.

That implies that you could be able to sell the same photograph a hundred, thousand more times.

8. <u>Launch A Blog Or A Youtube Channel.</u>

Although starting a blog might be difficult, blogging as a business concept has become increasingly popular as a passive income source.

You don't have to be a well-known personality on the internet to make money online.

Find a topic that is well-liked, even a small niche, and become an authority on it.

You'll need to develop a content library and attract readers initially, but as you establish a reputation for your engaging content, it can eventually generate a consistent income stream.

You could generate passive income from blogging or YouTube by:

- ❖ Promoting affiliate products.
- ❖ Publishing sponsored posts.
- ❖ Selling your goods.
- ❖ Advertise using Google AdSense.

What's best? You don't need any programming or design skills to start a blog. You can quickly launch a blog using a content management system and hosting service provider like *WordPress*.

You may utilize a free (or cheap) platform like *WordPress*, then use your excellent content to attract followers.

Your chances of becoming *"the"* person to follow are higher if your voice or area of interest is more distinctive. Then draw sponsors towards you.

You'll need to dedicate time to creating and promoting the content as well as developing an SEO marketing plan.

Be assured that it will reward your efforts, depending on how you monetize your blog, the return on investment may be as high as $30,000 per month.

9. Create A Dropshipping Store.

Even if you have a limited cash flow, dropshipping is one of the best ways to start earning money from wherever you are.

Some Dropshippers claim to earn more than $100,000 annually.

Dropshipping requires an initial time investment but is not a get-rich-quick scheme.

This business strategy entails setting up an online e-commerce store where clients may explore and purchase goods.

The interesting thing about dropshipping is that you don't have to physically see the goods you sell.

When you dropship, your supplier takes care of the entire process, including manufacturing, packaging, and delivery.

Also, there is less cash risk because you don't have to pay your supplier until your customers do.

The danger associated with investing in a product that has no market is another risk that you can avoid.

To identify popular items in various markets to offer in your shop, you can utilize a platform like *DSers*.

You may be able to generate a significant passive income and learn how to manage an e-commerce business depending on the product you choose and your pricing.

10.   <u>Acquire Stock Market Investments.</u>

The stock market is an excellent method to create enduring wealth, despite the steep learning curve and the possibility of confusion.

Thinking short-term rather than adopting a long-term view to achieve financial goals is a frequent mistake that most individuals make when investing in stocks.

Stock investments are meant to diversify your portfolio and lower risk.

You can accomplish this by purchasing exchange-traded funds (ETFs) and high-dividend stocks, both of which gradually increase your income over the long run.

You must create and fund a brokerage account before you can begin investing in the stock market.

11.   <u>Make A No-Code Application.</u>

Making the first-time commitment to creating an app may allow you to enjoy the benefits.

With today's no-code tools, even a beginner can make a simple to sophisticated software.

With the use of platforms like *WordPress, Appy Pie, Adalo, or Bubble*, it is possible to enter a market where there were 218 billion downloads in only 2020.

You must first choose between building a website or a mobile application.

Along with the app's idea (what market it will target and the problem it will address), monetization is another important consideration.

Consumers can download your application after it is made available to the general public, which allows you to earn money.

You can make Apps profitable by:

- ➢ Memberships.
- ➢ Advertisements.

- ➢ Download for a fee.
- ➢ A business model.

If you can create an app that appeals to your audience, it has a lot of potentials.

To maintain your app's appeal and relevancy when it grows in popularity or as a result of user feedback, you'll probably need to add more features.

12.   <u>Acquire REITs.</u>

Real estate investment trusts, or REITs, are companies that own and oversee profitable real estate.

It's a great opportunity for smaller investors to pool their funds to buy investments they otherwise wouldn't be able to afford.

Real estate investment trusts (REITs) offer an easy option to invest in real estate without having to deal with the hassle of property management.

REITs are a desirable alternative for investors seeking passive income since they generally distribute the bulk of their revenue in the form of dividends.

The average annual return for REIT investments over the last ten years was 9.5%.

If you have startup capital, REITs are a reliable passive income idea worth considering as a long-term investment.

Starting a business requires both upfront capital and extensive research. You don't want to enter into this venture haphazardly.

REITs can pass the majority of their profits to shareholders and pay little to no corporate income tax as a result of their unique legal structure.

REITs, like any other firm or dividend stock, can be acquired on the stock market.

Since the finest REITs often increase their dividend every year, you might build a rising stream of income over time. You will receive whatever the REIT pays you as a dividend.

Similar to dividend stocks, purchasing a single REIT might carry more risk than owning an ETF comprising many REIT stocks.

In addition to being far safer than purchasing individual stocks, a fund offers rapid diversification and yet offers a significant return.

13.   A Bond Ladder.

Bonds are an agreement between an investor and the bond guarantor - an organization, government, or government agency - to pay the investor a specific amount of interest over a specified timeframe.

The issuer pays the bondholder's principal when the bond matures at the end of the time frame.

A bond ladder is a collection of bonds that mature at various times for years.

The danger of reinvesting your money when bonds offer too-low interest payments can be minimized thanks to the staggered maturities.

A bond ladder is a well-known passive investment that has long been popular among retirees and those who are approaching retirement.

When the bond matures, you "stretch the ladder" by rolling the principle into a new set of bonds. Then you can relax and enjoy your interest payments.

Bonds with terms of one year, three years, five years, and seven years, for example, may be your first option.

When the first bond expires in a year, you will still have bonds with maturities of two years, four years, and six years.

You can use the recently matured bond's profits to purchase an additional one-year bond or to roll out a bond with a longer timeframe, such as an eight-year bond.

14.   <u>Open A High-Yield Saving Or Certificate Of Deposit Account.</u>

You can enjoy one of the best interest rates in the country while generating passive income by opening a high-yield certificate of deposit (CD) or savings account at an online bank.

Even better, you won't need to leave your house to earn money.

A simple approach to increasing your savings above what you would earn in a standard checking or savings account is by opening a high-yield savings account.

Although it won't be much, it's a quick method to begin earning passive income.

You should conduct a quick search for the best savings accounts or CD rates in the country to get the most out of your CD.

Since you may choose the best rate in the country, using an online bank is typically far more advantageous than using your local one.

And if your financial institution is backed by the FDIC (Federal Deposit Insurance Corporation) or any relevant government agency in your country of residence, you will still enjoy an assured return of principal up to $250,000.

15.   **<u>Rent Out Your House Briefly (Short-Let).</u>**

This easy method converts unused space into a source of income by utilizing space that you wouldn't otherwise use.

Consider renting out your existing apartment while you're away or if you're leaving town for an extended timeframe, going on vacation, or perhaps just wishing to travel.

You may choose your rental conditions and offer your room on any number of websites, including Airbnb.

You can list your space on quite a few sites, like Airbnb, and set the rental terms yourself.

Airbnb connects property owners with individuals who are searching for their next getaway.

There is a strong demand for your available space as an Airbnb host since people choose Airbnbs because they are usually less expensive than hotels.

You may purchase properties with the sole intent of renting them if you want to increase your Airbnb income.

However, you should know that setting up a rental apartment frequently involves work. Before renting out your spare space, you might need to furnish or remodel it.

If you rent to a tenant who may stay for a few months, you'll receive a payment for your efforts with minimal extra work.

16.   Lease Your Vehicle.

You can utilize more than just your free space to generate passive income.

Using a service like *Turo*, you can also lease out your vehicle.

If you already use your vehicle for *Uber*, you may sign up with *Carvertise* or *Wrapify* to make extra money while you travel around the city.

Another alternative is to look for somebody who needs a vehicle for *Uber or Lyft.*

So rather than actively cruising all over in your spare time, you can pull up a Netflix show while your vehicle works for you.

17. Stake Cryptocurrency.

When done passively, investing in many cryptocurrencies, sometimes known as *"staking crypto"*, can be a terrific method to earn anywhere between 5% and 10%.

Consider it similar to collecting interest on your savings, but with more rewards.

What is the first step? Learn about proof-of-stake cryptocurrencies and how to access a crypto wallet first.

To decide which cryptocurrency to invest in, you'll need to educate yourself on the many options available.

Once you're ready, crypto exchanges like *Coinbase, Binance, or Kraken* can be excellent places for purchasing cryptocurrency.

After that, all that's left to do is wait for the returns on your assets and keep an eye on them.

The more informed you are about the world of cryptocurrencies, the wiser your investment choices will be.

Remember that staking cryptocurrency carries risks of its own, just like any investment.

You'll also need to devote a lot of time upfront studying your options so you can make smart investments.

18.   Sell Your Designs Online.

Online design marketplaces like *99designs, ThemeForest, or Creative Market* are excellent options.

These platforms offer a built-in market that is already hungry for design materials, regardless of whether you utilize a website builder to create website themes, logos, branding resources, templates, drawings, or even fonts.

The $13.1 billion sector of graphic design in the US is constantly expanding. Thankfully, securing a passive piece of that pie can also be simple.

For instance, you would have to apply and wait for approval if you desire to start selling designs on *Creative Market.*

From there, you get your retail store, where you may begin offering your exclusive creations for sale.

19.   <u>**Record Audiobooks.**</u>

Someone has to create audiobooks. Why can't you be that individual?

They pay a majority of audiobook narrators with royalties, so if you establish yourself in the field, it is easy to generate passive income in this manner.

There are a few things you need to get right before you can successfully create passive revenue from audiobooks.

These comprise learning:

⇨   Ways to audition.
⇨   Appropriate narration techniques.
⇨   What area of interest (niche) you'll pursue.
⇨   Some editing skill sets.

You don't have to struggle by yourself. Several platforms make it simpler to start and secure your first few jobs.

Visit websites like *ACX* to discover what you need to succeed in the field.

20.   <u>Create And Sell Spreadsheets.</u>

Some of us are spreadsheet experts by nature. If so, you might use your knowledge of spreadsheets to generate passive income.

There is a market that will pay you to generate spreadsheets of many types, including budgeting, profit estimates, habit tracking, and P&L spreadsheets that business owners don't want to construct from scratch.

You may make these spreadsheets using *Excel or Google Sheets.*

Pair the *Digital Downloads app* and a *Shopify business* together to create a passive income stream that is ready to generate cash.

However, you do need to get customers to your storefront for that to happen.

You can likewise distribute and sell these spreadsheets on *Amazon Kindle.*

CHAPTER 4

Which Source Of Passive Income Is The Best?

Which passive income source is ideal relies on several variables, but the most crucial ones are your financial situation, the size of the total opportunity, your ability and interest in the business, the time investment required, and your hunger for success.

The more competitors there are and the smaller the chance of success, generally speaking, the lower the entry barriers.

Therefore, you must assess the potential in light of these factors and determine which passive income approach suits you the most.

However, it can be advantageous to possess a natural talent and a keen interest in the field you choose to pursue because these traits can serve as sources of inspiration when times are rough.

For individuals who are starting with little money as well as those who have no money at all, there are opportunities for passive income.

How Can I Get Passive Income Without Any Money?

If you're starting with little to no money, you'll need to rely mostly on your time investment to get you through, at least until you start saving up some money.

That implies concentrating on sources of passive income that benefit from the following characteristics:

a) <u>An area in which you are an authority:</u> Here, you may turn your skills in areas like freelancing, design, software coding, and others into a meaningful product or service for customers.

b) <u>An upfront work-intensive opportunity:</u> You'll need an opportunity that involves putting in some time or effort, like developing a course, building an influencer profile, or other alternatives.

In essence, until you have enough money to increase your opportunities, you are substituting your time for your lack of capital.

What Are Some Ways I Can Use Money To Make Passive Income?

You can find additional passive investment opportunities with money. You have both the opportunity described above and a new range if you have money to invest in a passive opportunity.

To benefit from the following passive income sources, you need money:

a) <u>Acquiring dividend-paying stocks or REITs:</u> Although investing in stocks requires an initial financial commitment, the rewards are among the most passive income streams available.

b) <u>Bonds or CDs are good ways to save:</u> Purchasing bonds or Certificates of Deposit (CD) is another pure passive activity.

If that's what you'd like to do, you may utilize your money here to generate money with little to no work on your side. Of course, you may pair your cash with a significant time investment to enter a market that is much more rewarding.

How Many Sources Of Income Ought One To Have?

There is no *"one size fits all"* approach when it comes to generating income streams.

Your financial situation and future financial goals should determine how many sources of income you have. However, having a handful is an excellent place to start.

Greg McBride, CFA, chief financial analyst at Bankrate, says that using many lines in the water can increase your chances of landing fish. *"In addition to the earned income produced by your human capital, rental properties, income-generating assets, and company initiatives are fantastic ways to diversify your revenue stream."*

Naturally, you'll want to make sure that working on a new passive income stream isn't taking your attention away from your current income sources.

To make sure you're selecting the finest opportunities for your time, you should optimize your efforts.

CONCLUSION

Reduce Your Passive Income Taxes

A passive income can be an excellent approach for making extra money, but you'll also incur tax obligations.

But by establishing yourself as a business and opening a retirement account, you may lessen the tax burden while still planning for the future.

However, this method won't work for all of these passive strategies, and to be eligible, your business must be legitimate.

Get a tax identification number for your company by registering with the IRS.

Then get in touch with a broker, such as *Charles Schwab or Fidelity*, who can start a retirement account for self-employed individuals.

Choose the retirement account type that would suit your needs best.

The *Solo 401(k)* and the *SEP IRA* are two of the most widely used choices. You can deduct this year's taxes if you put the money in a traditional *401(k) or SEP IRA*.

The *Solo 401(k)* is fantastic because you may contribute up to 100% of your earnings, up to the yearly limit, to the account.

The *SEP IRA*, however, only permits contributions at a 25 percent rate. Additionally, the *Solo 401(k)* allows you to contribute an additional contribution of up to 25% of your business revenues.

If you're considering taking this path, compare the two account types or look at the top retirement plans for self-employed.

The Path To Financial Freedom

There are only so many hours in the day, so finding ways to increase your income might provide you the flexibility you need to take your business to the next level.

Whatever stage you're at, having additional income sources with different underlying economics might allow you the opportunity to explore it. It can include *"going on a vacation," "hiring more staff,"* or *"placing an order for new products."*

The secret to unlocking riches is *creating passive income streams*.

You can't truly use leverage if you are continuously exchanging your time for money.

If you truly want to be financially successful, your money needs to generate more money.

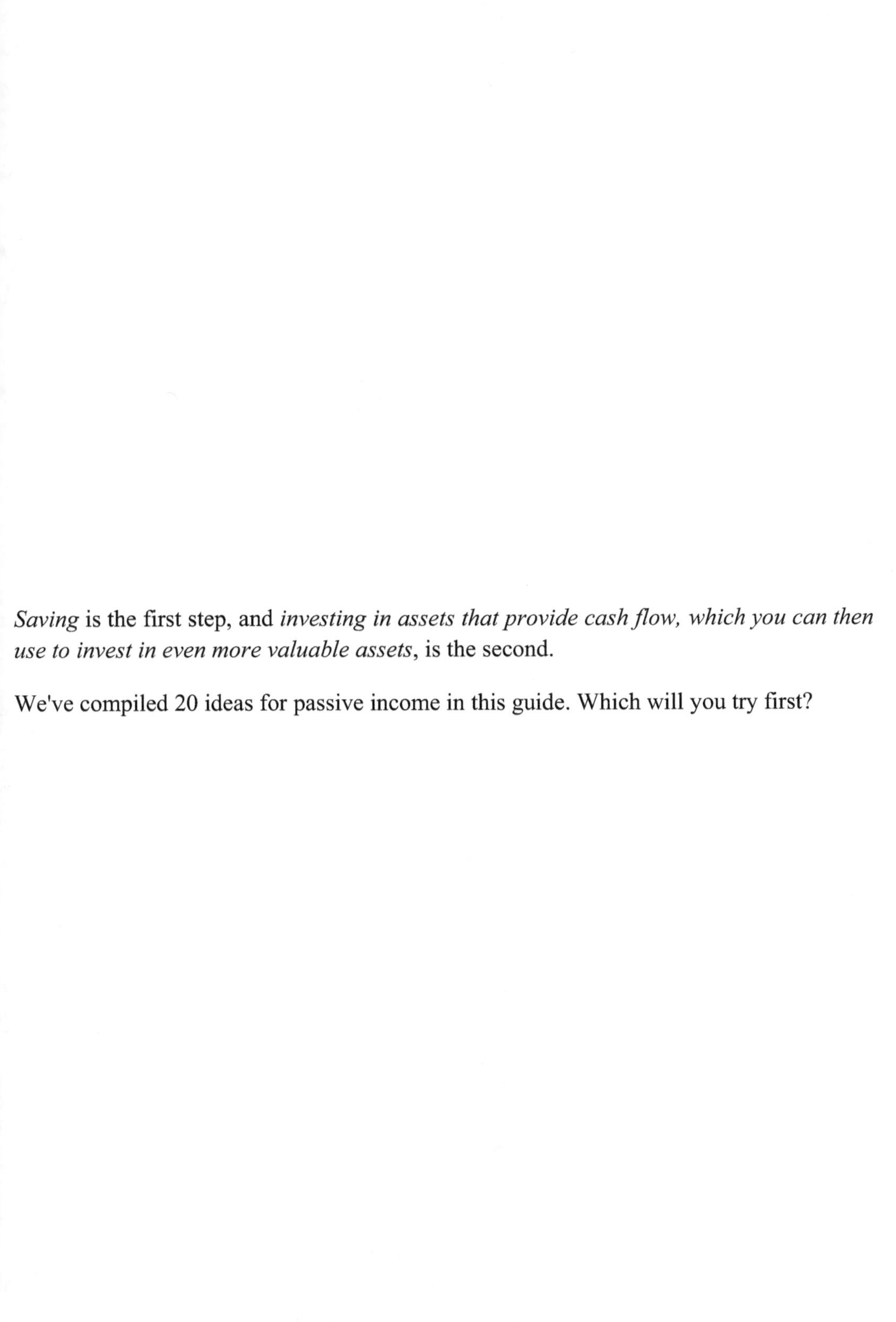

Saving is the first step, and *investing in assets that provide cash flow, which you can then use to invest in even more valuable assets*, is the second.

We've compiled 20 ideas for passive income in this guide. Which will you try first?

www.ingramcontent.com/pod-product-compliance
Lightning Source LLC
Chambersburg PA
CBHW071238140726
47996CB00007B/2665